Contents

Christmas themed worksheets…………………… 1

Christmas and New Year in Spain……………… 8

Colour by number using colours in Spanish……. 14

Christmas & pet animals………………………… 20

Word searches…………………………………… 24

Christmas games (board game style) …………… 28

Christmas & New year cards to colour…………. 34

Spanish bookmarks to colour……………………. 45

Spanish - English word list……………………… 47

Answer section…………………………………… 48

La Navidad (Christmas)

Escribe las palabras en español: (Write in Spanish the words:)

1)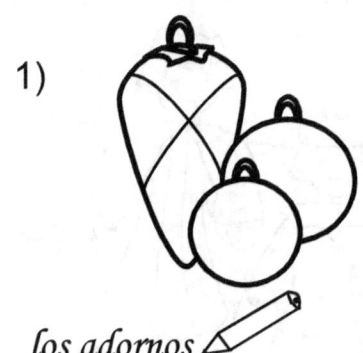
los adornos

un reno	a reindeer
un árbol	a tree
un regalo	a present
una estrella	a star
los reyes	the kings
los adornos........	the decorations
Papá Noel	Father Christmas

2)
_____

3)
_____

4)
_____

6)
_____

5)
_____

7)
_____

Un calcetín de Navidad (a Christmas sock)

1 = uno   2 = dos   3 = tres   4 = cuatro   5 = cinco   6 = seis   7 = siete

Diseña un calcetín de Navidad y dibuja dentro de el:
(Design a Christmas sock and draw on it:)

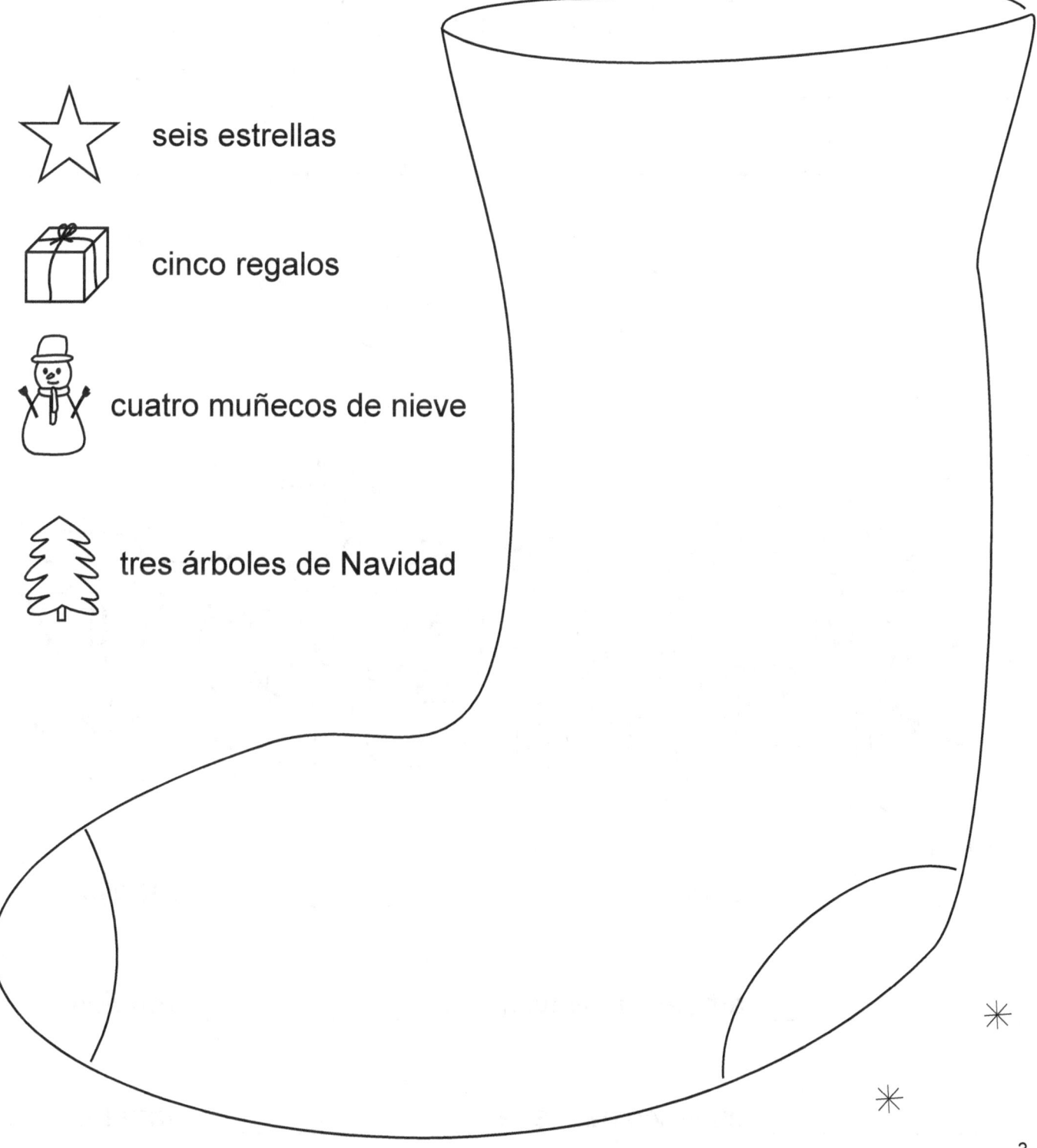

seis estrellas

cinco regalos

cuatro muñecos de nieve

tres árboles de Navidad

¿Cuántos hay? (How many are there?)

1 = uno   2 = dos   3 = tres   4 = cuatro   5 = cinco   6 = seis   7 = siete

cuatro

_____ renos _____ estrellas

_____ árboles de Navidad _____ regalos

_____ muñecos de nieve _____ tarjetas

Los árboles (trees)

Dibuja la cantidad adecuada de árboles:
(Draw the correct number of trees:)

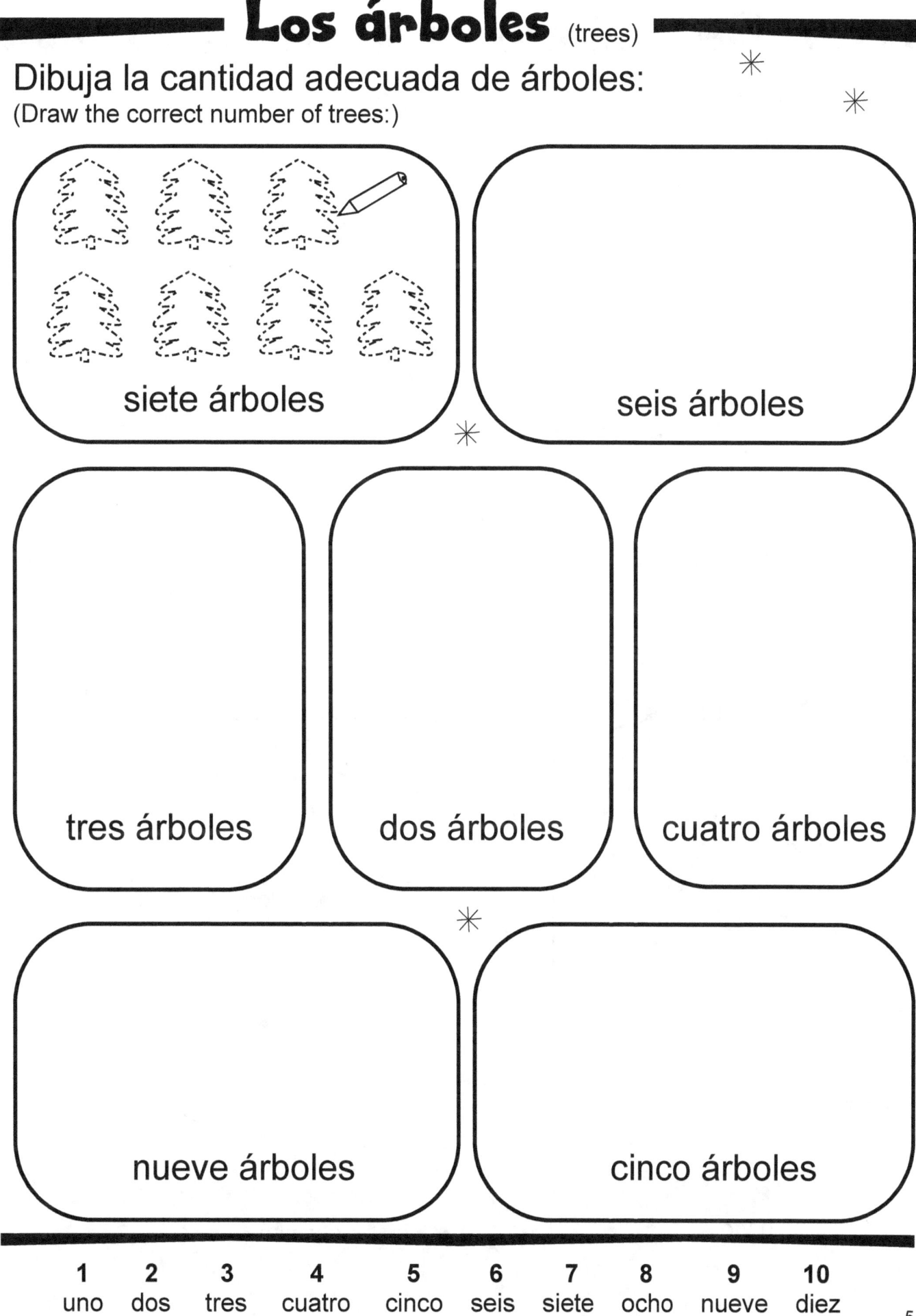

siete árboles		seis árboles
tres árboles	dos árboles	cuatro árboles
nueve árboles		cinco árboles

1	2	3	4	5	6	7	8	9	10
uno	dos	tres	cuatro	cinco	seis	siete	ocho	nueve	diez

Un muñeco de nieve (a snowman)

Une los puntos en el orden correcto:
(Join the dots in the correct order:)

dieciocho •   • diecinueve

diecisiete •————————————• veinte
dieciséis •   • veintiuno
     quince •————————————• veintidós

catorce •

trece •————————• veintitrés
doce •   • uno

once •

     • dos

diez •

     • tres

nueve •   • cuatro

•   •
ocho   cinco
   siete   seis

1	uno
2	dos
3	tres
4	cuatro
5	cinco
6	seis
7	siete
8	ocho
9	nueve
10	diez
11	once
12	doce
13	trece
14	catorce
15	quince
16	dieciséis
17	diecisiete
18	dieciocho
19	diecinueve
20	veinte
21	veintiuno
22	veintidós
23	veintitrés

Symmetry

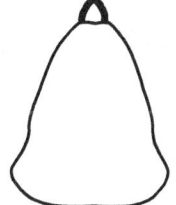

Haz el otro lado del dibujo igual al primer lado:
(Make the other side of the picture the same as the first side:)

Usa estos colores: (Use these colours:)

- ☐ gris
- ○ naranja
- △ amarillo
- ♡ rojo
- ◇ verde
- ⬭ azul
- △ lila

La Navidad en España (Christmas in Spain)

Nochebuena (Christmas Eve)

On the 24th December Spanish families have a special meal. Typical meals vary region to region and by family preferences. Popular choices include **el pescado** (fish), **el cordero** (lamb) and **los mariscos** (shell fish).

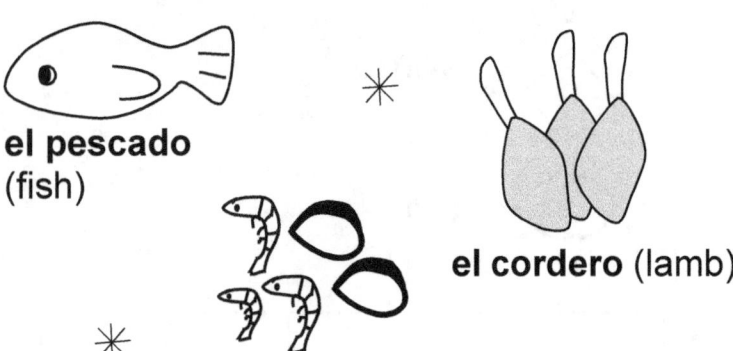

el pescado (fish)

el cordero (lamb)

los mariscos (shell fish).

un belén (A nativitiy scene)
Many Spanish people have a nativity scene in their houses. And throughout Spain, you will see nativity scenes the size of Santa's grottos in the centres of Spanish towns and cities.

El turrón is a nougat which is often eaten at Christmas. It is made with sweet almonds.

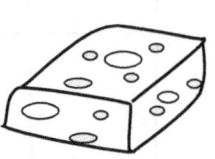

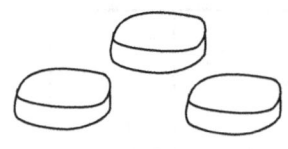

Los polvorones are crumbly shortbread style cakes, and are typically eaten over the festive period.

To wish someone "Happy Christmas" in Spanish, say **Feliz Navidad** (The final z in feliz has a th sound):

Feliz Navidad

Feliz Navidad

La Navidad en España (Christmas in Spain)

Copia las palabras y haz los dibujos:
(Copy the words and do the drawings:)

 un belén

un belén

_____

 el pescado

_____

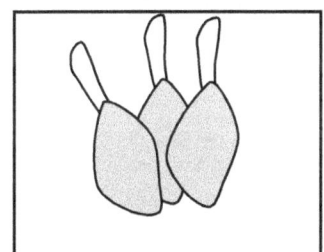 el cordero

_____

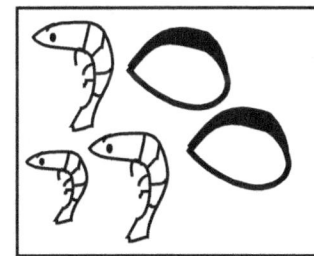 los mariscos

_____

 el turrón

_____

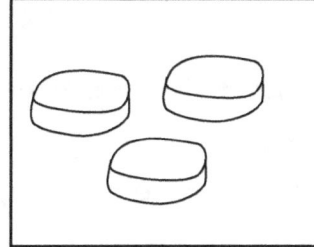 los polvorones

_____

La Nochevieja (New Year's Eve)

In Spain, at midnight many Spanish people believe it's lucky to eat twelve grapes. (One grape for each chime of the clock at midnight.)

Each person needs 12 grapes, but the children below don't have enough grapes! How many grapes are they missing? Write the number of grapes each child needs in Spanish:

Tengo sólo = I only have   necesito = I need   más = more

a) Tengo sólo cinco uvas. Necesito __siete__ más.

b) Tengo sólo ocho uvas. Necesito _____ más.

c) Tengo sólo diez uvas. Necesito _____ más.

d) Tengo sólo siete uvas. Necesito _____ más.

e) Tengo sólo seis uvas. Necesito _____ más.

1	2	3	4	5	6	7	8	9	10	11	12
uno	dos	tres	cuatro	cinco	seis	siete	ocho	nueve	diez	once	doce

El seis de enero (The sixth of January)

The sixth of January in Spain is a very important date in the calendar, as the Spanish celebrate the arrival of **los reyes magos** (the three kings) to visit Jesus.

On the evening of the 5th January people line the streets to see a fantastic parade where **caramelos** (sweets) are thrown for the children to catch.

Regalos (presents) are often exchanged on the 6th January and there is a special meal. A typical cake is called un **rosco de reyes.**

Colorea: (colour:)

los reyes en azul, marrón y rojo

dos regalos en rosa

tres regalos en lila

cuatro caramelos en rojo

cinco caramelos en verde

tres caramelos en lila

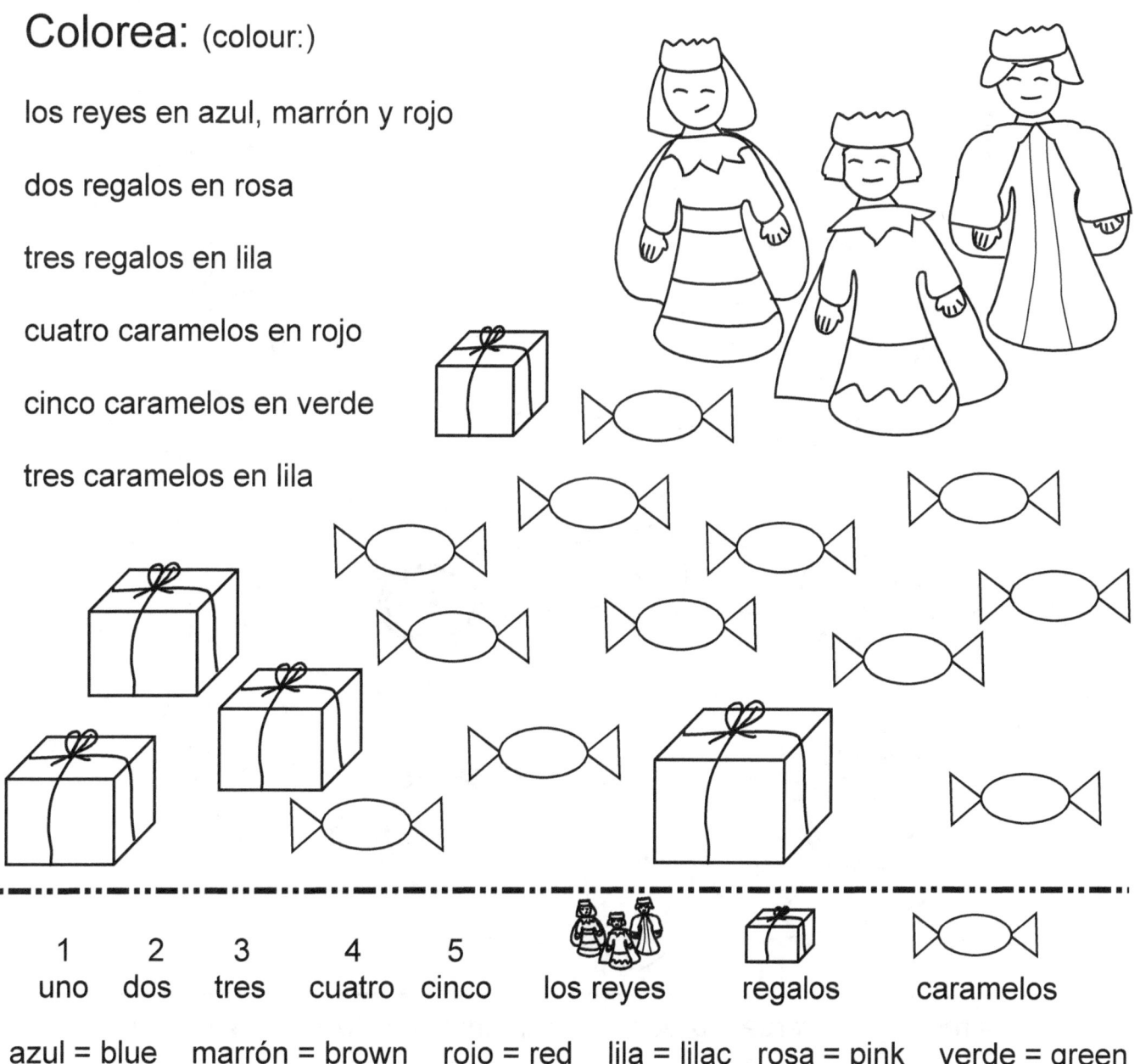

1	2	3	4	5			
uno	dos	tres	cuatro	cinco	los reyes	regalos	caramelos

azul = blue   marrón = brown   rojo = red   lila = lilac   rosa = pink   verde = green

El rosco de reyes

On the 6th January it's typical in Spain to eat El rosco de reyes. It's a cake shaped like a crown. And on the top there are lots of jellies or fruit in place of the jewels. Colour los roscos de reyes in the correct colours:

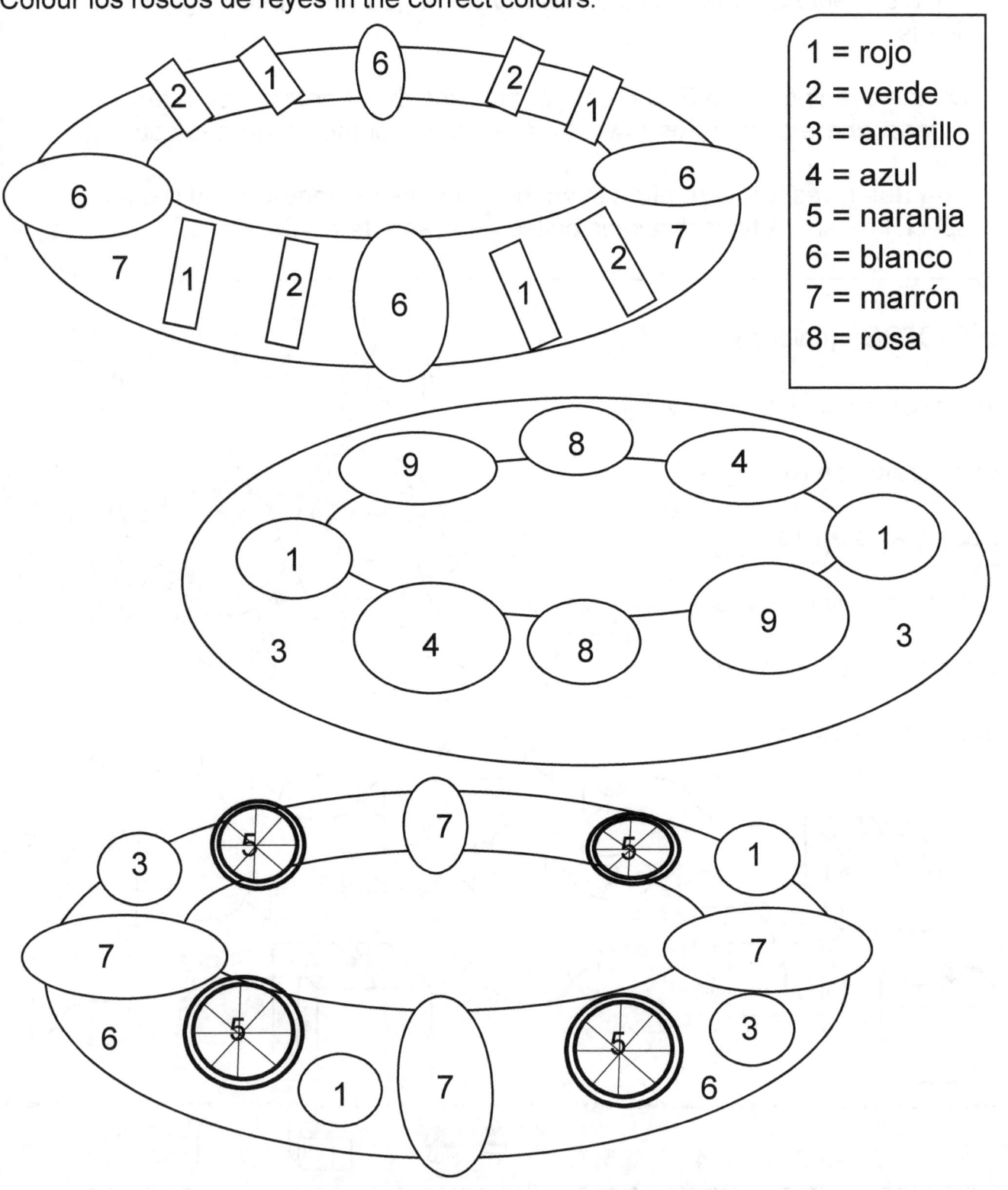

1 = rojo
2 = verde
3 = amarillo
4 = azul
5 = naranja
6 = blanco
7 = marrón
8 = rosa

rojo = red   verde = green   amarillo = yellow   azul = blue
blanco = white   marrón = brown   rosa = pink   naranja = orange

Los reyes (the kings)

Colorea los reyes: (Colour the kings:)

1 = rojo
2 = verde
3 = amarillo
4 = negro
5 = azul
6 = blanco
7 = marrón
8 = lila
9 = rosa
10 = gris
11 = naranja

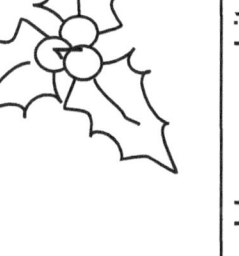

rojo = red   verde = green   amarillo = yellow   azul = blue   blanco = white
marrón = brown   lila = lilac   rosa = pink   negro = black   gris = grey   naranja = orange

Un árbol de Navidad (a Christmas tree)

Colorea el dibujo: (Colour the picture)

1 = rojo
2 = verde
3 = amarillo
4 = negro
5 = azul
6 = blanco
7 = marrón
8 = lila
9 = rosa
10 = gris
11 = naranja

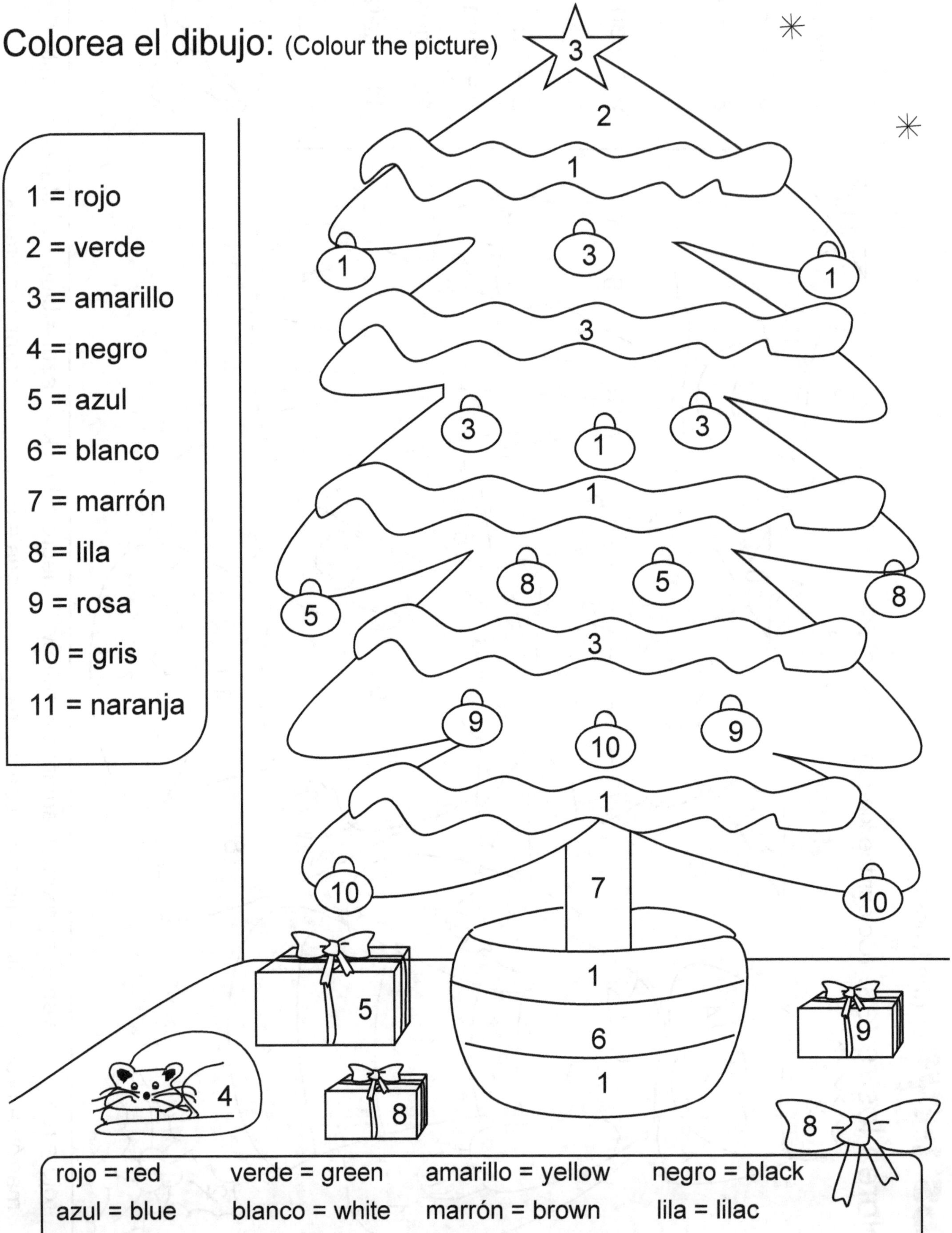

rojo = red	verde = green	amarillo = yellow	negro = black
azul = blue	blanco = white	marrón = brown	lila = lilac
rosa = pink	gris = grey	naranja = orange	

Los regalos de Navidad
(Christmas presents)

Colorea el dibujo: (Colour the picture)

1 =	rojo
2 =	verde
3 =	amarillo
4 =	negro
5 =	azul
6 =	blanco
7 =	marrón
8 =	lila
9 =	rosa
10 =	gris
11 =	naranja

 rojo = red verde = green amarillo = yellow negro = black
azul = blue blanco = white marrón = brown lila = lilac
rosa = pink gris = grey naranja = orange

Los adornos de Navidad (Christmas decorations)

Colorea los adornos de Navidad: (Colour the Christmas decorations:)

1 = rojo
2 = verde
3 = amarillo
4 = negro
5 = azul
6 = blanco
7 = marrón
8 = lila
9 = rosa
10 = gris
11 = naranja

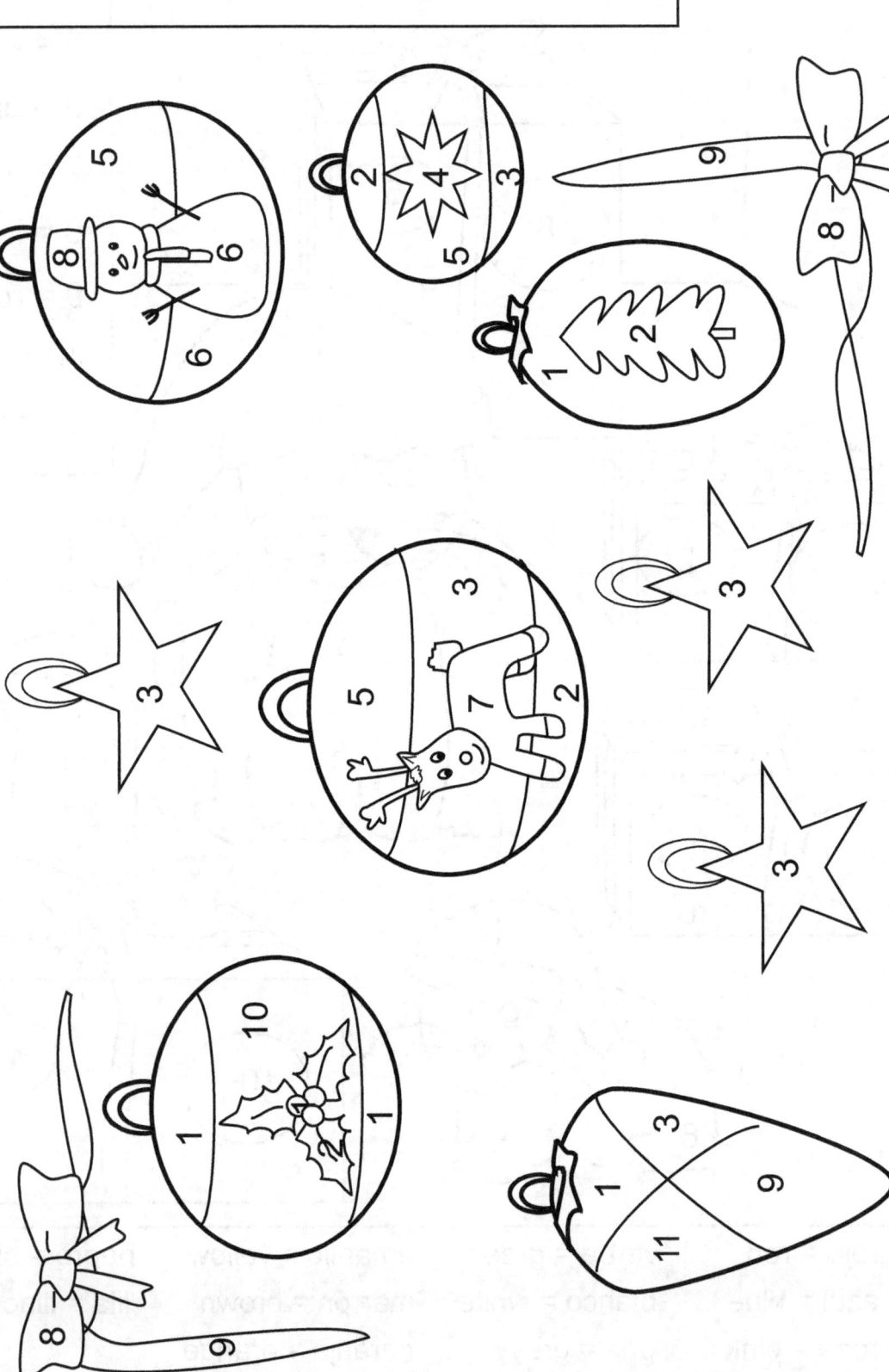

rojo = red   verde = green   amarillo = yellow   negro = black   blanco = white
marrón = brown   lila = lilac   rosa = pink   gris = grey   naranja = orange

Las velas de Navidad (Christmas candles)

Colorea el dibujo: (Colour the picture)

1 = rojo	2 = verde	3 = amarillo	4 = negro
5 = azul	6 = blanco	7 = marrón	8 = lila
9 = rosa	10 = gris	11 = naranja	

  rojo = red verde = green amarillo = yellow negro = black
azul = blue blanco = white marrón = brown lila = lilac
rosa = pink gris = grey naranja = orange

Un oso de peluche

(A teddy bear)

Colorea el oso de peluche:
(Colour the teddy bear)

1 = rojo
2 = verde
3 = amarillo
4 = negro
5 = azul
6 = blanco
7 = marrón
8 = lila
9 = rosa
10 = gris
11 = naranja

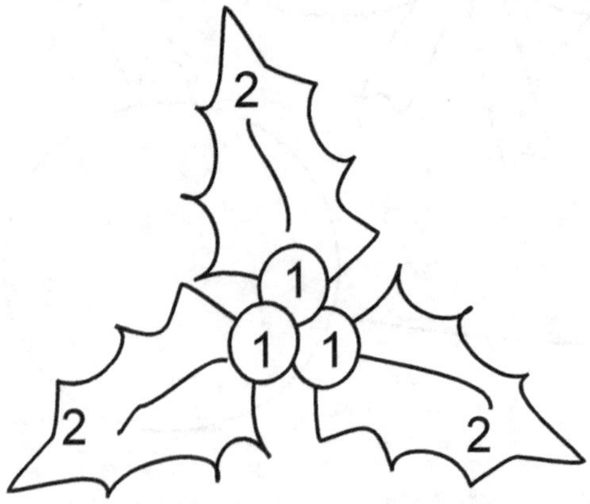

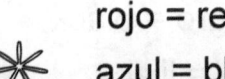

rojo = red	verde = green	amarillo = yellow	negro = black
azul = blue	blanco = white	marrón = brown	lila = lilac
rosa = pink	gris = grey	naranja = orange	

Un jersey de Navidad (a Christmas jumper)

Escribe en español el nombre del animal que veas en cada jersey:
(Write in Spanish the animal you see on each jumper:)

1)
un gato

2)

_____

3)

_____

4)

5)

_____

6)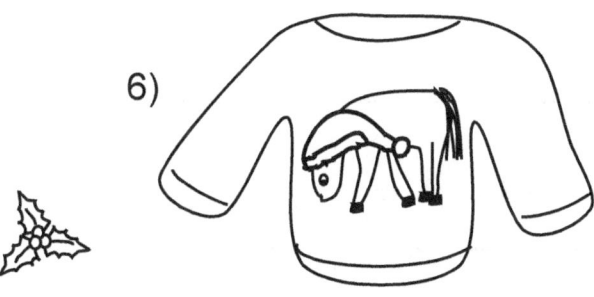

un gato	= a cat
un perro	= a dog
un caballo	= a horse
una tortuga	= a tortoise
un conejo	= a rabbit
un pájaro	= a bird

_____

Me gustaría tener una mascota

(I would like to have a pet)

1) Dibuja la mascota que quieren tener los niños:
(Draw the pet the children would like to have:)

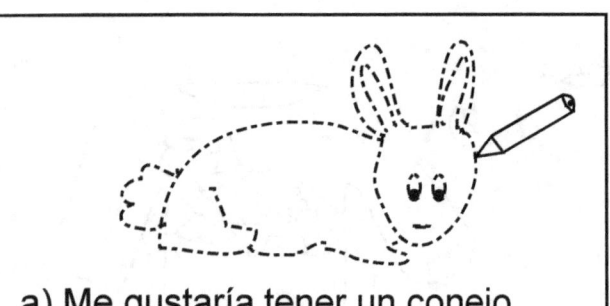

a) Me gustaría tener un conejo.

b) Me gustaría tener un pez.

c) Me gustaría tener una serpiente.

2) Imagínate que quieres tener estas mascotas. (Imagine you want to have these animals). **Escribe las frases** (Write the sentences)

Me gustaría tener un pájaro.

1) _____ .

2) _____ .

3) _____ .

4) _____ .

| un gato = a cat | un perro = a dog | un caballo = a horse | un pez = a fish |
| un conejo = a rabbit | un pájaro = a bird | una serpiente = a snake | |

¿Te gustan los animales? (Do you like animals?)

los gatos = cats	los perros = dogs	los caballos = horses
los peces = fish	los conejos = rabbits	los pájaros = birds
las tortugas = tortoises	los hámsters = hamsters	las serpientes = snakes

Imagine **Papá Noël** needed to know what your favourite animals were, in case he was getting you something with a picture of an animal on it.

Write in Spanish the animals you like in the box with me gustan. If there are any animals you don't like, write them in the box with no me gustan. (The animals are written in the plural, as we are talking about animals in general and not just one particular pet.)

Me gustan
(I like)

No me gustan
(I don't like)

La Navidad en España (Christmas in Spain)

Busca estas palabras: (Find these words:)

 los REYES

 el BELÉN

 el TURRÓN

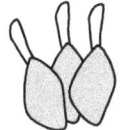 el CORDERO

 el PESCADO

 los MARISCOS

 las UVAS

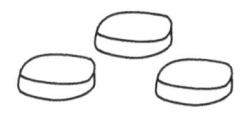 los POLVORONES

NOCHE BUENA   NOCHEVIEJA

 In Spanish there are four different ways of saying our word "the": el, la, los, las. These words do not appear in the word search.

Los colores (colours)

Busca estas palabras: (Look for these words:)

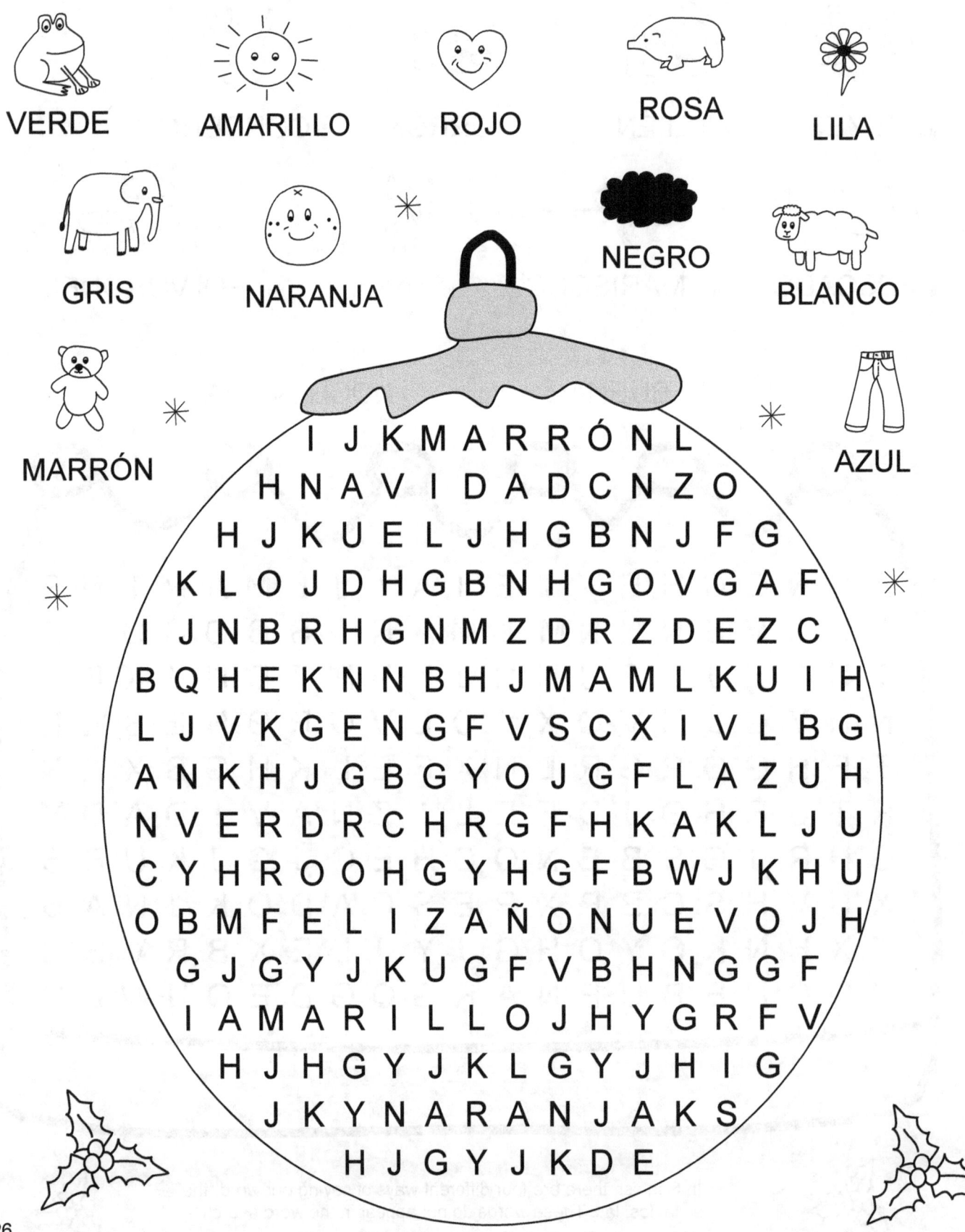

VERDE AMARILLO ROJO ROSA LILA

GRIS NARANJA NEGRO BLANCO

MARRÓN AZUL

```
I J K M A R R Ó N L
H N A V I D A D C N Z O
H J K U E L J H G B N J F G
K L O J D H G B N H G O V G A F
I J N B R H G N M Z D R Z D E Z C
B Q H E K N N B H J M A M L K U I H
L J V K G E N G F V S C X I V L B G
A N K H J G B G Y O J G F L A Z U H
N V E R D R C H R G F H K A K L J U
C Y H R O O H G Y H G F B W J K H U
O B M F E L I Z A Ñ O N U E V O J H
G J G Y J K U G F V B H N G G F
I A M A R I L L O J H Y G R F V
H J H G Y J K L G Y J H I G
J K Y N A R A N J A K S
H J G Y J K D E
```

Los animales (animals)

Busca estas palabras: (Look for these words:)

el PERRO
el CABALLO
el PÁJARO
el CONEJO
la TORTUGA
el PEZ
la SERPIENTE
el GATO
ANIMALES
MASCOTA

```
        O S E R H K J X
      P T K H C A B A L L O U
      M S A A N I M E H L J V E H
      P E G R O C H N T O R T U G A C N
      S E R R N P H K P E R H B G A T H C
      C H R B E E B E H K H K L O W N Z O
      K E J N B Z E S E R P I E N T E B N X
      P A N M E L E M Z H E H X L E N M E E P
          M A S C O T A Q J M Á
                      Z E O B J
                      E N A A
                      M K N R
                          I O
                          M E H
                          A C X
                          L E B
                          E V P
                          S C H
```

In Spanish there are four different ways of saying our word "the": el, la, los, las. These words do not appear in the word search.

27

Lets play some games!

To play the Christmas games on the following pages, you can either photocopy the games, play the games directly in the book, or with an adult carefully cut the games out of the book.

If you are playing the games directly in the book it may be useful to put something like a book or a pencil case on the top of the book to hold the page down.

Things you will need:

For counters you can use things like rubbers, cubes or counters from other games you have. Just check the counters you use aren't too big for the games. If you have a piece of paper or card, you could even make your own counters!

Some games require a dice, but if you don't have one with an adult you could cut a piece of paper into small pieces, and write the numbers from one to six on them. Then, instead of rolling a dice you could randomly pick a card with numbers 1 to 6 on.

Remember to say the Spanish words whilst you play the games!

For this game you will need a dice and a counter for each player. Start at salida, roll the dice and count that number of spaces. Say in Spanish what is in the space you land on. Take turns to roll the dice. To win, arrive first at Llegada.

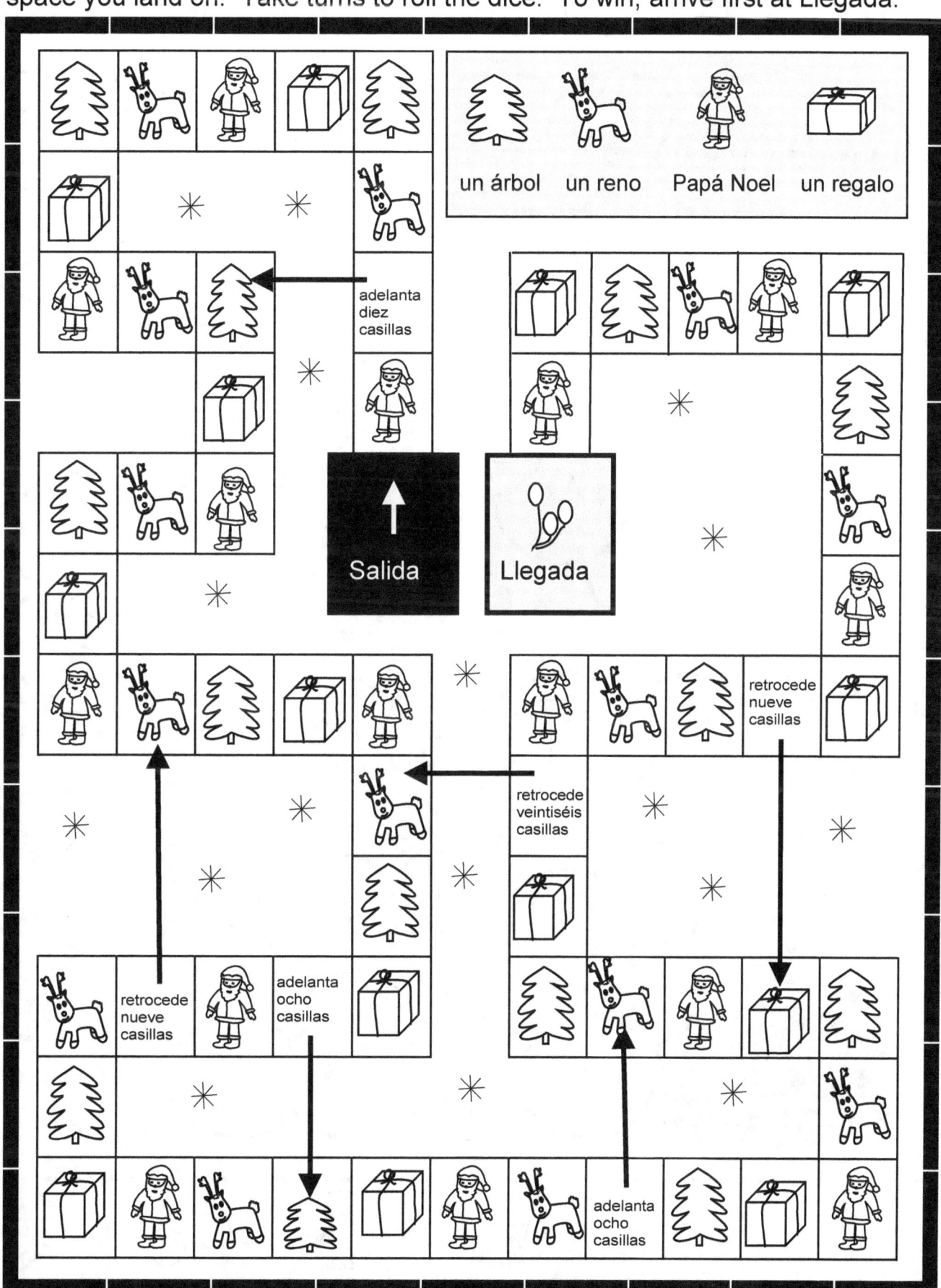

Start at salida, roll the dice and count that number of spaces. Say the word you land on in Spanish. If you land on un reno move forward an extra 2 spaces. If you land on un árbol miss a go next turn. To win, arrive first at llegada.

 una estrella    un regalo    un reno    Papá Noel   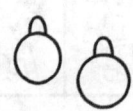 adornos    un árbol

Each person / team needs 15 coloured cubes or counters.

Say the word pictured in Spanish as you place your counter or cube. To win you have to get 4 in a row (vertically, horizontally or diagonally).

 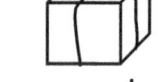    

una estrella   un regalo   un angel   una tarjeta   un reno   Papá Noel

 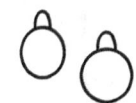

un árbol de Navidad   un muñeco de nieve   adornos

Start at salida, roll the dice and count that number of spaces. Go down a snake or up a ladder if there is one in the final space you land on. Say the Spanish word for the food you land on. To win, arrive first at Llegada.

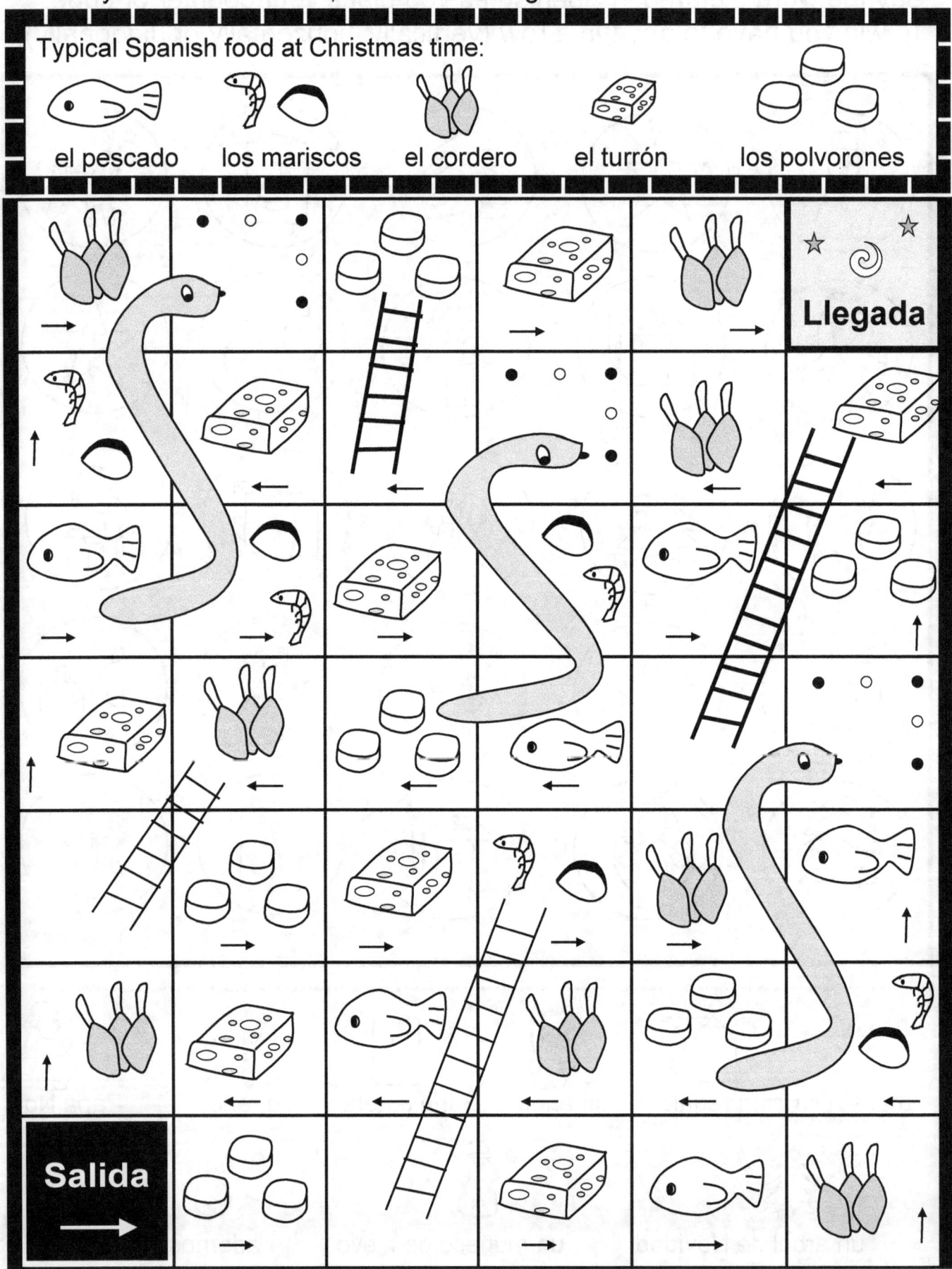

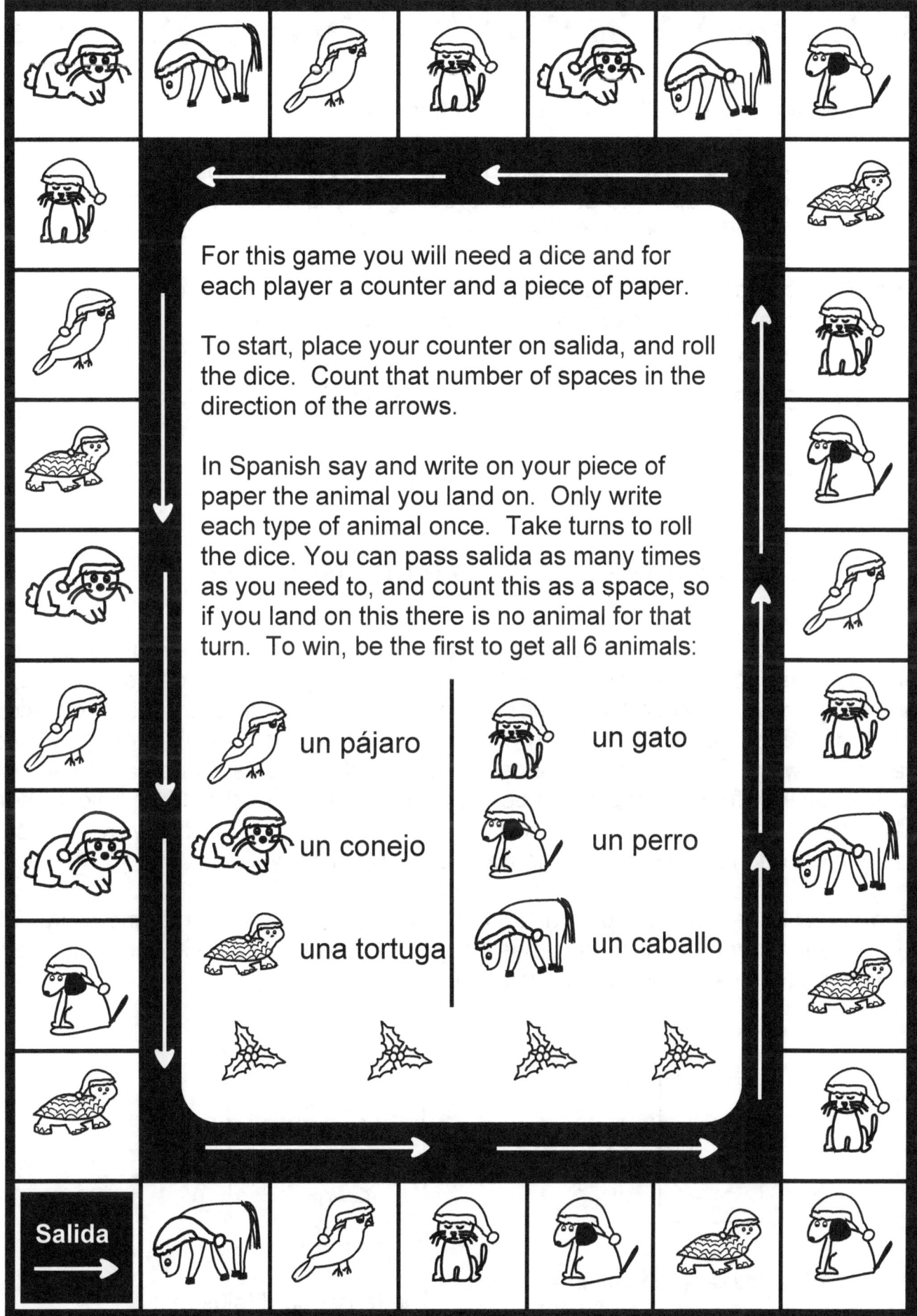

Lets make Spanish Christmas cards !

There are two sizes of Christmas cards in this book:

The small size is designed to be folded in 4, so even when on paper the Christmas cards should stand up. The Christmas greeting may look like it's upside down, but when you fold the card in 4, the greeting is inside the card and the correct way up!

The larger cards fold in 2, and ideally would be photocopied onto card. You can write your own greeting in the card. Here are some useful phrases:

Feliz Navidad ………….. Happy Christmas

y……………………..…….. and

Feliz año nuevo ……..…. Happy New year

If you want, you can photocopy the Christmas cards to make numerous cards. To avoid photocopying and getting black lines from the photocopier on the cards, photocopy first one copy on white paper, then check if you have any black lines from the photocopier. If you do, cover the black lines with white paper before photocopying the quantity of cards you want. To be sure the Christmas card will fold correctly use a ruler to check where half way from the top would be. The front of the card should be below where half way is. If for some reason your photocopy hasn't turned out that way, rearrange the original on the photocopier, and do another photocopy.

If you don't have a photocopier, ask an adult if they can cut the Christmas cards out of the book for you. All the Christmas cards that appear in this book are followed by a blank page in case you want to use them as cards.

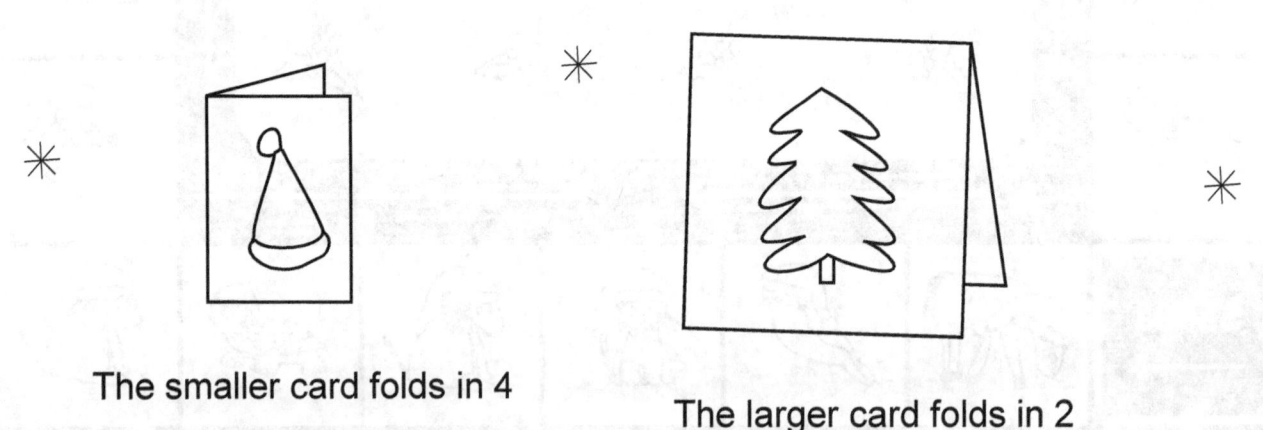

The smaller card folds in 4

The larger card folds in 2

Feliz Navidad
y
Feliz año nuevo

Feliz Navidad

Feliz Navidad
y
Feliz año nuevo

Feliz Navidad

To make the 4 book marks either photocopy this page (ideally onto card) or with an adult cut this page out of the book. Colour the pictures and the border, then with an adult cut out the bookmarks.

Bookmark 1: Feliz Navidad

Feliz Navidad (Happy Christmas)

- una estrella
- Papá Noel
- un angel
- un árbol
- un regalo
- los reyes
- adornos
- un reno
- un muñeco de nieve

Feliz año nuevo (Happy New year)

Bookmark 2: los colores

- verde
- amarillo
- marrón
- blanco
- gris
- naranja
- rojo
- azul
- negro
- lila
- rosa

Bookmark 3: los animales

- un pez
- un perro
- un gato
- un pájaro
- un caballo
- un conejo
- una tortuga
- una serpiente

Bookmark 4: Hola

Hola (Hello)

- uno
- dos
- tres
- cuatro
- cinco

por favor (please)

gracias (thank you)

Adiós (Good bye)

	Spanish		English		Spanish		English
	adornos		decorations		naranja		orange
	amarillo		yellow	la	Navidad		Christmas
un	angel	an	angel		necesito		I need
los	animales	the	animals		negro		black
un	árbol de Navidad	a	Christmas tree	la	Nochebuena		Christmas Eve
	azul		blue	la	Nochevieja		New Year's Eve
un	belén	a	Nativity scene		nueve		nine
	blanco		white		ocho		eight
	Buenos días		Good morning		once		eleven
un	caballo	a	horse	un	oso de peluche	a	teddy bear
una	campana	a	bell	un	pájaro	a	bird
	caramelos		sweets		Papá Noel		Father Christmas
	cinco		five	un	perro	a	dog
un	conejo	a	rabbit	el	pescado		fish
el	cordero		lamb	un	pez	a	fish
	cuatro		four	los	polvorones		crumbly shortbread cakes
	diez		ten	un	regalo	a	present
	doce		twelve		regalos		presents
	dos		two	un	reno	a	reindeer
	España		Spain	los	reyes magos	the	three kings
una	estrella	a	star		rojo		red
	Feliz año nuevo		Happy New Year		rosa		pink
	Feliz Navidad		Happy Christmas		seis		six
un	gato	a	cat	una	serpiente	a	snake
	gris		grey		siete		seven
	Hola		Hello	una	tarjeta	a	card
un	jersey	a	jumper		tengo		I have
	lila		lilac		Tengo ___ años		I am ___ years old
los	mariscos		shell fish	una	tortuga	a	tortoise
	marrón		brown		tres		three
una	mascota	a	pet	el	turrón		nougat
	Me gustaría		I would like		uno		one
	Me llamo		My name is		uvas		grapes
un	muñeco de nieve	a	snowman		verde		green

Answers

Page 2

1) los adornos 2) un árbol 3) un reno 4) Papá Noel 5) los reyes
6) una estrella 7) un regalo

Page 3

The following should be drawn on the Christmas sock:

seis estrellas = six stars   cuatro muñecos de nieve = four snowmen
cinco regalos = five presents   tres árboles de Navidad = three Christmas trees

Page 4

cuatro renos   siete estrellas   tres árboles de Navidad   seis regalos
dos muñecos de nieve   cinco tarjetas

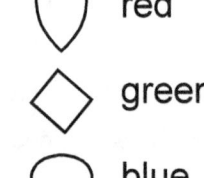

Page 5

siete árboles = seven trees
seis árboles = six trees
tres árboles = three trees
dos árboles = two trees
cuatro árboles = four trees
nueve árboles = nine trees
cinco árboles = five trees

Page 6

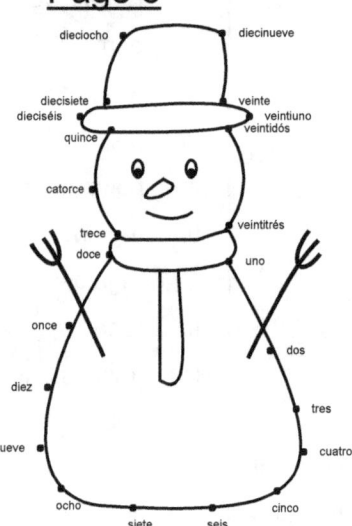

Page 7

☐ grey   ♡ red
◯ orange   ◇ green
△ yellow   ⬭ blue
           ✦ lilac

Page 10

a) siete   b) cuatro   c) dos
d) cinco   e) seis

Page 11

The picture should be coloured as follows:
The kings in blue, brown and red
2 presents in pink   3 presents in lilac
4 sweets in red   5 sweets in green   3 sweets in lilac

Page 12

1 = red   2 = green   3 = yellow   4 = blue   5 = orange   6 = white   7 = brown   8 = pink

Pages 13-20

1 = red   2 = green   3 = yellow   4 = black   5 = blue   6 = white   7 = brown
8 = lilac (light purple)   9 = pink   10 = grey   11 = orange

Page 21

1) un conejo   2) una tortuga   3) un pájaro   4) un perro   5) un gato   6) un caballo

Page 22

1a) a rabbit   b) a fish   c) a snake

2a) Me gustaría tener un pájaro   b) Me gustaría tener una tortuga
 c) Me gustaría tener un caballo   d) Me gustaría tener un gato

Page 24

(Word search in Christmas tree shape containing: REGALO, PAPÁNOEL, TARJETA, ESTRELLA, REYES, FELIZNAVIDAD, FELIZAÑONUEVO, ÁRBOLDENAVIDAD, MUÑECODENIEVE, plus additional letters)

Page 26

(Word search in circle shape containing: MARRÓN, NAVIDAD, ROJO, AZUL, BLANCO, NEGRO, LILA, VERDE, ROSA, FELIZAÑONUEVO, AMARILLO, GRIS, NARANJA)

Page 25

(Word search containing: NOCHEVIEJA, MARISCOS, BELÉN, POLVORONES, FELIZNAVIDAD, PESCADO, NOCHEBUENA, plus additional letters)

Page 27

(Word search in Santa hat shape containing: CABALLO, TORTUGA, SERPIENTE, MASCOTA, CONEJO, PÁJARO, ANIMALES, PEZ, PERRO, GATO, plus additional letters)

© Joanne Leyland 2021
This book may be photocopied for class or home use by the purchasing individual or institution.
It may not be reproduced digitally.

Also available by Joanne Leyland:

French
Young Cool Kids Learn French
Sophie And The French Magician
Daniel And The French Robot - Books 1, 2 & 3
Jack And The French Languasaurus - Books 1, 2 & 3
Cool Kids Speak French (books 1, 2 & 3)
French Word Games - Cool Kids Speak French
40 French Word Searches Cool Kids Speak French
First 100 Words In French Coloring Book Cool Kids Speak French
French at Christmas time
On Holiday In France Cool Kids Speak French
Cool Kids Do Maths In French
Un Alien Sur La Terre
Le Singe Qui Change De Couleur
Tu As Un Animal?

Italian
Young Cool Kids Learn Italian
Cool Kids Speak Italian (books 1, 2 & 3)
Italian Word Games - Cool Kids Speak Italian
40 Italian Word Searches Cool Kids Speak Italian
First 100 Words In Italian Coloring Book Cool Kids Speak Italian
On Holiday In Italy Cool Kids Speak Italian
Un Alieno Sulla Terra
La Scimmia Che Cambia Colore
Hai Un Animale Domestico?

German
Young Cool Kids Learn German
Cool Kids Speak German (books 1, 2 & 3)
German Word Games - Cool Kids Speak German
40 German Word Searches Cool Kids Speak German
First 100 Words In German Coloring Book Cool Kids Speak German

Spanish
Young Cool Kids Learn Spanish
Cool Kids Speak Spanish (books 1, 2 & 3)
Spanish Word Games - Cool Kids Speak Spanish
40 Spanish Word Searches Cool Kids Speak Spanish
First 100 Words In Spanish Coloring Book Cool Kids Speak Spanish
Spanish at Christmas time
On Holiday In Spain Cool Kids Speak Spanish
Cool Kids Do Maths In Spanish
Un Extraterrestre En La Tierra
El Mono Que Cambia De Color
Seis Mascotas Maravillosas

The word search editions have 40 topics in each book. The word searches are in fun shapes. Pictures accompany the words to find.

The first 100 words colouring book editions have 3 or 4 words per page, and are ideal for those who like to colour as they learn.

The stories in a foreign language have an English translation at the back.

If you like games, you could try the word game editions.

The holiday editions have essential words & phrases in part 1. And in part 2 there are challenges to use these words whilst away.

For more information on the books available, and different ways of learning a foreign language go to https://learnforeignwords.com

www.ingramcontent.com/pod-product-compliance
Lightning Source LLC
Chambersburg PA
CBHW081356080526
44588CB00016B/2519